JESUS WENT TO HEAVEN FOR ME AND FOR YOU

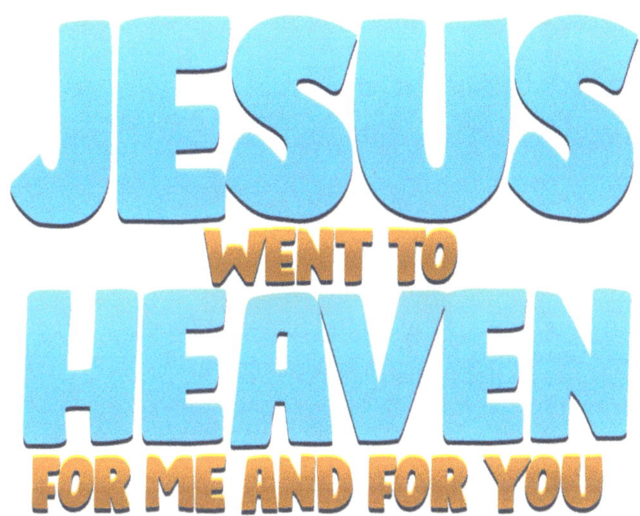

WRITTEN BY **EVA MAYLE**

ILLUSTRATED BY ONIEL RODRIGUEZ

FOR ME FOR YOU
BOOKS

I dedicate this book in memory of my parents, who always kept us in church and prayed for the seven of us. To my children, who I love so very much and pray for always. And to my Savior, Jesus Christ, who has never given up on me.

JESUS WENT TO HEAVEN FOR ME AND FOR YOU.

HE DID IT BECAUSE HE LOVES US,
AND HE DID IT FOR FREE.

HE SPEAKS THROUGH HIS
WORD FOR OUR LITTLE
EARS TO HEAR,
AND PROMISES TO LOVE US
AND TO STAY SO NEAR.

HOLY BIBLE
HOLY BIBLE

HE GIVES US OUR HUGS EACH DAY AND NIGHT FROM MOMMIES AND DADDIES WHO HOLD US TIGHT.

HE SENDS OUT THE SUN
TO BRIGHTEN OUR DAY,
SO WE CAN GO OUT
WITH OUR FRIENDS TO
PLAY.

HE SENDS OUT THE
MOON WHEN BEDTIME
DRAWS NEAR,
AND WE CAN BE SURE
THERE'S NOTHING TO
FEAR.

WENT TO HEAVEN

REMEMBER, HE LOVES YOU WHEN BAD OR GOOD,
BUT BEING YOUR BEST IS WHAT YOU SHOULD DO.

SO BEFORE YOU LAY
YOUR HEAD TO SLEEP,
SAY A PRAYER,
"MY SOUL TO KEEP."

AND DREAM OF OUR
JESUS, WHO LOVES YOU
TOO
BECAUSE HE WENT TO
HEAVEN FOR ME AND FOR
YOU.

* 9 7 9 8 9 8 5 4 4 1 2 2 2 *